Vintage FASHION

OTTILIE GODFREY

ARCTURUS

For Eleanor Barbara Beatrice, with my love

The publisher would like to thank the following for permission to reproduce photographs: Derek Bayes/Lebrecht Music & Arts: 48 (right); Bettmann/Corbis: 6, 10, 14, 16 (left), 17, 19 (left), 20, 23, 27, 29 (left), 33, 48 (left), 55 (right), 56 (right), 62 (both), 68 (bottom), 71, 72, 91 (top), 104, 118, 120 (bottom); Buyenlarge/Getty Images: 46 (right); Cat's Collection/Corbis: 61; CinemaPhoto/Corbis: 49, 78; Condé Nast Archive/Corbis: front cover, 7, 13, 18, 28, 30–31, 32 (left), 34, 35 (top), 36, 38, 39, 40, 41, 43, 44, 46 (left), 47, 50, 52, 53, 54, 56 (left), 57, 59, 63, 64, 65, 66 (left), 67, 69, 70, 73, 74, 77, 80 (left), 81, 82 (both), 83, 84 (left), 85, 86, 87 (left), 88, 89, 90, 91 (bottom), 92–93, 95, 96, 98, 99 (both), 100, 105 (both), 108 (both), 110, 111, 115, 116 (both), 117, 119, 121, 123 (bottom), 124 (bottom), 125, 126 (top), 127; Corbis: 15 (bottom); Getty Images: 103; Gianni Dagli Orti/Corbis: 12; De Agostini/Lebrecht Music & Arts: 19 (right), 23 (top), 29 (right), 35 (bottom); Julio Donoso/Sygma/Corbis: 113; Hulton Archive/Getty Images: 107; Hulton-Deutsch Collection/Corbis: 51, 80 (right), 87 (right), 101; Interfoto/Lebrecht Music & Arts: 37 (bottom); Harry Langdon/Getty Images: 109; Lebrecht: 26; Mirrorpix/Lebrecht Authors: 84 (right); David Montgomery/Getty Images: 114; Michael Ochs Archives/Getty Images: 97; Popperfoto/Getty Images: 102; PoodlesRock/Corbis: 15 (top); RA/Lebrecht Music & Arts: 11, 16 (right), 21; Roger Ressmeyer/Corbis: 122; John Springer Collection/Corbis: 9, 22, 25, 37 (top); Sunset Boulevard/Corbis: 60, 66 (right), 68 (top); TAL RA/Lebrecht Music & Arts: 55 (left); Topfoto: 79; Underwood & Underwood/Corbis: 45, 75; Pierre Vauthey/Sygma/Corbis: 106, 120 (top), 123 (top), 124 (top), 126 (bottom).

ARCTURUS

This edition published in 2013 by Arcturus Publishing Limited
26/27 Bickels Yard, 151–153 Bermondsey Street,
London SE1 3HA

ISBN: 978-1-84858-977-3
AD002472EN

Editing and picture research: Patience Coster

Printed in Singapore

Contents

The Cycle of Fashion

Throughout history, fashion has served as a marker of class and wealth. The rulers of Ancient Rome introduced sumptuary laws to ensure that the garments people wore reflected their social standing – it was an easy way to tell who was worth speaking to! Meanwhile, clothes have always courted controversy. The Emperor Honorius issued a decree prohibiting men from wearing 'barbarian' trousers in Rome, on pain of death. An extreme form of sartorial control, it presumably kept troublemakers at bay. With the mods and rockers of the 1960s, the police had only their powers of arrest to rely on!

WHY STYLES EVOLVED

This book looks at twentieth century vintage fashion – from the Roaring Twenties to the Exuberant Eighties – and examines how and why styles evolved. Fashions are often linked to a change in social mood. After the First World War, the 'bright young things' wore rule-breaking outfits to match their rule-breaking

behaviour. In 1947, after the Second World War, the New Look swished its skirts in reaction to stiff upper lips, ration books and frugal fashions. Similarly, the 'don't mess with me' wide-shouldered suits and ostentatious jewellery of the Eighties contrasted with the 'let it all hang out' free-flowing peasant frocks and attitude of the Seventies.

Although the twentieth century built up the walls of haute couture, it was also responsible for tearing them down. The democratizing effect of two world wars, the emancipation of women and the surge in mass production meant that the exclusive world of designer fashion began to lose its jealously guarded dominance. Since the Sixties, the cycle of fashion has been spinning ever faster – clothes now become fashionable, then out-of-date and then 'retro' at breakneck pace. Slavish followers of fashion find themselves spending a lot of money on clothes that quickly end up as landfill. To make matters worse, many of the fashions available on the high street are unoriginal and of dubious quality. Buying vintage is a

good way to avoid the mediocrity of the chain stores. It means you can revel in owning a garment carefully made from quality fabric and, if you are lucky, by a name synonymous with style.

NOT JUST A LOAD OF OLD FROCKS!

Those fashion designers whose work has lasted found a way to tap into the public consciousness to produce iconic pieces. In many ways they defined the contours of the twentieth-century female form. Coco Chanel's Little Black Dress, quilted bags, twinsets and pearls, slacks and sportswear are all classics that have been collectable for decades. Other designers whose vintage items are sought-after today include Jeanne Lanvin, Madeleine Vionnet, Elsa Schiaparelli and Christian Dior, as well as the more affordable Ossie Clark, Vivienne Westwood, Jean Paul Gaultier, Barbara Hulanicki (Biba) and Christian Lacroix.

Wearing vintage fashion transports you back in time and provides a connection with people from the past. By wearing clothes or jewellery owned by a favourite female friend or relative you may feel closer to them in some way. Most vintage and retro clothing was made at a time when clothes were expected to last. You may be delighted to find that your Fifties frock or Sixties trouser suit is much better tailored and constructed than anything you could buy today.

Perhaps the recent rise in the popularity of vintage fashion is connected with our search for identity and meaning in this young and, as yet, unshaped twenty-first century. With the twentieth century now firmly behind us, we can assess and make sense of it with ease. We can also conveniently compartmentalize it into decades – as, indeed, we have done for this book!

It would be misleading to claim that fashion can explain the complexities of history, but it can give us glimpses of people's personalities, moods and tastes and their reactions to a changing world. What could be a more potent reminder of the people who inhabited the twentieth century than the opportunity to – literally – walk a mile in their shoes?

The Roaring Twenties

The iconic Twenties image beloved of fancy-dress partygoers is that of the flapper, with fringed frock, pale stockings, ostrich-feathered headband and several strands of pearls to twirl while dancing the frenetic Charleston. In the years following the First World War, this idea of the 'fast life' was applauded as society's expectations shifted to embrace a more optimistic era – the 'Jazz Age'. Streamlined cars, cocktails, new music, smoking . . . the younger generation eagerly grasped whatever recreational activities came along after the horrors of the previous decade. Meanwhile, many British women had gained fulfilment from actively participating in the war effort, and those over the age of 30 had won the vote in 1918 (with all adult women to follow in 1928). These social advances meant that women were not about to return meekly to their previous place in society, let alone to the restrictive clothes of the Edwardian era.

Women literally and metaphorically stepped out of their corsets and the restrictions of the old order. An outfit in the Twenties typically weighed a tenth of an Edwardian ensemble. Severe boned corsets were replaced by light camisoles and drawers. Silk stockings, a luxury, were replaced by 'artificial silk', or rayon stockings that could be purchased by the majority rather than the few. Rayon stockings were available in 'natural', black or white.

At a time when most women players competed in outfits covering almost the entire body, tennis champion and style icon 'La Divine' Suzanne Lenglen caused a sensation by appearing on court in a Jean Patou calf-length pleated shift and sleeveless sweater. Soon many women were baring their arms and foreheads. Hair was bobbed *à la* Louise Brooks or shingled like Clara Bow, the 'It Girl' who with Brooks came to epitomize the flapper in films. Some flappers cut their hair in a schoolboyish Eton crop. In millinery, the cloche hat vied with the bandeau to be the most fashionable form of headdress.

Clothes became far less cumbersome and more androgynous. The new silhouette was straighter and freer with long lines. The most fashionable style of dress was a simple chiffon or crepe sheath made of less fabric than ever before, which meant that cut was paramount. Madeleine Vionnet crafted beautifully designed dresses cut diagonally to the grain of the fabric, which enabled them to cling to the body. This bias cut would dominate the construction of women's clothes into the Thirties.

In 1922, the discovery of Tutankhamun's tomb led to a worldwide obsession with all things Ancient Egyptian. Dresses with stiff folds in the front and festooned with Egyptian motifs were worn with scarab style jewellery. But the future of fashion was decisively determined by the 'garçonne' collection of one Gabrielle 'Coco' Chanel. Her skirts were calf-length and very simple – almost masculine – in design, with the waistline dropped to the hips. Chanel also showed nautical jackets, cardigan suits and jersey trousers. The absence of overt decoration on the clothes was compensated for by costume jewellery. Long strings of beads or pearls (excellent imitation

OPPOSITE American actress Nancy Carroll with Marcel-waved hair and feather-trimmed clothing and accessories that sum up the Jazz Age.

The 'It Girl' Clara Bow in a sheer, sleeveless, sequinned sheath with a chunky Ancient-Egyptian-inspired bracelet.

pearls came on to the market at this time) were worn both day and evening. Chiffon scarves appeared as daywear, worn either around the neck or attached to the dress. Chanel used simple fabrics such as jersey (until this time generally regarded as an inferior cloth) which lent themselves to mass production. It could be argued that the 'garçonne' collection, along with innovations in textile machinery, paved the way for the democratization of fashion and the hasty adaptation of haute couture for the high street. Chanel's first Little Black Dress was feted in *American Vogue* in 1926 as a 'uniform for all women of taste'.

In 1909, Sergei Diaghilev's dance company, the Ballets Russes, moved to Paris, an event that laid the foundations for the Art Deco period to come. In 1925, the Exposition Internationale des Arts Décoratifs et Industriels Modernes had a worldwide impact, resulting in a wave of new thinking and making an immediate impact on taste. Consumer goods, including clothing, became purer, simpler and more streamlined – frippery was a thing of the past. Ukranian artist-designer Sonia Delaunay made clothes for her Futurist friends, creating kaleidoscopic patterns in geometric or abstract designs that still look

A 1924 colourized newspaper illustration shows suits by Coco Chanel –
note the dropped waist and uncluttered lines.

fresh today. Italian fashion designer Elsa Schiaparelli's 1928 sweater with a *trompe l'oeil* scarf around the hips, joining a real one at the side, foreshadowed her later famous Surrealist pieces.

By the middle of the decade, the Charleston craze meant that women who wanted to do this modern dance eschewed the traditional heavy ballgown. Dresses quickly became shorter and sheerer, with shoestring straps and side splits, and were loaded with beads, fringes or sequins to accentuate the movement of the body. They were generally sleeveless, so women kept themselves warm with long-fringed silk shawls that were often heavily embroidered with Egyptian or geometric Deco symbols. Some shawls were fur-trimmed, a fashion brought to the West by the Ballets Russes.

After the initial shock of their dramatic rise, hemlines continued to fluctuate, even becoming asymmetrical in 1928 when Jean Patou dropped the back hem only. However, towards the end of the decade hemlines were on their way down again. By the time of the Wall Street Crash of 1929, they had plummeted along with the economy. The Roaring Twenties fell silent.

Pierre Brissaud 1920.

ABOVE Voted the 'best-dressed woman in America' in the 1920s, Irene Castle shot to fame with her husband Vernon as a ballroom dance pairing. Her grace and exquisite posture made her a perfect fashion model. Here she shows off a 1921 dress by Lucile (Lady Duff Gordon) in pale taffeta. It is worn over an underskirt of cream tulle and Valenciennes lace with a matching hat, pale stockings and satin ribbon-laced shoes.

OPPOSITE A 1920 fashion illustration from the influential French magazine *La Gazette du Bon Ton* displays the stylish way to dress when calling on friends in the afternoon. The woman's dress features a fashionable exotic influence in the embroidery on the Cossack-style sleeves, belt, hem and hat. The girls wear frocks with embroidered sleeves and cloche hats over bobbed hair.

RIGHT An illustration from *Elite Style* magazine shows the early Twenties' elongated funnel lines which skimmed the bust and waist. These fashions meant that elaborate and uncomfortable corsetry was no longer required. The parasol was used to protect the skin from an unfashionable suntan, but it was also deployed for decorative and flirting purposes.

OPPOSITE Mrs James Lawrence Breese of Southampton and New York photographed on holiday in Hot Springs, Virginia, March 1922. She wears a straw hat over bobbed hair and a blouse with a Peter Pan collar under a long-line sweater tied at the hips – the perfect spring vacation outfit for a young socialite. A matching two-tone belt, Mary Jane shoes, a simple pendant and white gloves, teamed with an early version of the tote bag, complete the look.

BELOW A glimpse of stocking may have been shocking for some Twenties tennis fans, but with her bare arms and Jean Patou wardrobe, French champion and first female tennis celebrity Suzanne Lenglen became the woman to watch on and off court. At the time, the French press nicknamed this flamboyant sports star 'La Divine'.

LEFT French designer Jeanne Lanvin captured every conceivable fashion element in this 1925 dress of Nile-green panné (crushed) velvet with a dropped waist and tea-length full gathered skirt. The shoes and jewellery are kept simple, allowing the hip-accentuating circle of fur and pearlized embroidery to take centre stage.

ABOVE An illustration by John La Gatta for a 1925 magazine shows the new tailored style with a shorter length, double-breasted dress and typical Twenties fur-trimmed wrap coat, both by Molyneux. The two-tone court shoes pick up the red of the hat and tie in with the coat and dress trim.

OPPOSITE Greta Garbo in her first American film, *Torrent* (1926). Max Rée designed this sumptuous black, white and gold fur opera coat to demonstrate the rise of Garbo's film character from farmer's daughter to stage star.

OPPOSITE Poolside fashion, 1928: the female model wears a two-piece bathing suit consisting of a black-and-white-striped sleeveless sweater-style top over black side-buttoned shorts with matching striped bathing socks, all by Schiaparelli.

RIGHT This vermilion 'paño lency' (felt) cloche hat from c.1925 has a black satin lining and black-and-orange grosgrain band. A matching felt flower accentuates the dropped-back brim.

BELOW Joan Crawford seen here in an Adrian lamé and bugle-beaded Deco detail costume for the Cedric Gibbons' designed movie *Our Dancing Daughters* (1928). Crawford was one of the few Hollywood actresses of the Twenties who managed to cast off her flapper image and make the transition to the 'talkies'.

LAVER'S LAW

James Laver was a British author, art historian, television presenter, 'iconographer' and educator. Between 1938 and 1959, he was Keeper of Prints, Drawings and Paintings at the Victoria and Albert Museum in London. In addition to this roll call of occupations, Laver was an early and influential fashion historian. His interest in fashion stemmed from a desire to date works of art accurately through the clothing of their subjects. He developed a theory, known as 'Laver's Law', which stated that a garment 'ten years before its time' tended to be regarded as 'indecent', whereas a garment ten years behind the curve was viewed as 'hideous'. Laver's Law is still used as a guide to the fashion trend lifecycle. Laver asserted that it takes 30 years for a fashion to become of interest. An example of this is the way in which Forties fashions were revisited and reinterpreted in the Seventies.

Laver also displayed a talent for light verse. His comic poem 'The Women of 1926' is a revealing glimpse into the impulses and preoccupations of the 'bright young things' of the Twenties.

We've silken legs and scarlet lips,
We're young and hungry, wild and free,
Our waists are round about the hips
Our skirts are well above the knee
We've boyish busts and Eton crops,
We quiver to the saxophone.
Come, dance before the music stops,
And who can bear to be alone?

ABOVE The daughter of the Bolivian minister to France, resplendent in a 1929 Patou-designed wedding gown made from acres of satin trimmed with hand-embroidered seed pearls and strass (crystal). The family heirloom veil of *point d'angleterre*, the bride's 'something old', was vintage even then!

OPPOSITE This flapper costume of straight-waisted gown, evening gloves, long strings of pearls and feather boa, realized by Chanel in 1928, still looks modern today. Coco Chanel pioneered costume jewellery, 'masculine' tailoring for women, suntans, ballet pumps, the Little Black Dress and much more. Chanel remains a byword for expensive elegance.

Fash-399

OPPOSITE With her black, precision-bobbed hair and sultry eyes, silent movie star Louise Brooks was described as the 'living embodiment of the flapper ideal'. As a star both of American and European films, Brooks specialized in 'wild girl' roles starting, aged 20, with *A Social Celebrity* (1926) and progressing to *Pandora's Box* (1929). She was also a talented dancer and an intelligent and witty writer. The famous Brooks bob would eventually be designated one of the ten most influential hairstyles in history.

ABOVE RIGHT This Twenties clutch bag in conker-coloured lizard skin has a beaten silver metal and semi-precious stone clasp and optional fine link chain. During this time, it became acceptable (and quickly fashionable) for women to re-apply lipstick in public, so mirrors started being incorporated into the flaps or inside pockets of handbags.

RIGHT Tamara de Lempicka, Polish artist and creator of some of the most iconic images of the era, photographed arriving in New York harbour in 1929. She is dressed in the height of fashion in a knee-length fur coat, 'masculine' tailored suit, felt cloche hat, day clutch bag and heeled two-tone brogues.

The Inventive Thirties

While to the casual observer it looked as though everyone was having fun, the Roaring Twenties were wretched for all but the rich. However, they were nothing compared to the next decade, dubbed by Groucho Marx the 'Threadbare Thirties', which witnessed the beginning of the Great Depression. Not everyone was ruined by the Wall Street Crash but, as photographer Cecil Beaton noted in 1930, 'Even if you haven't lost money, you have to pretend you have.' Restraint became the byword for this era.

In 1932, Chanel slashed her prices by half and managed to stay in business. Despite this shrewd move, the Thirties were to be the decade of another designer, Elsa Schiaparelli, Chanel's arch-rival. Schiaparelli's surreal visual trickery was truly original – take, for instance, the 'chest of drawers' suit, the lobster dress and the whimsical shoe hat – but she broke the mould when she pioneered the zip fastener (sometimes left deliberately on show) and used 'insect' buttons and 'clashing' colours, often incorporating her own 'shocking pink'. In 1939, Schiaparelli also designed the eminently practical 'alert suit', an all-in-one ensemble and forerunner of the 'siren suit' that was to be worn by many, including Winston Churchill, during the Second World War.

Even among the wealthy, there were few British women who could afford Parisian haute couture. During the Thirties, London designers such as Norman Hartnell and Charles James came to prominence, while Creed's restrained tweed suits represented the height of elegant day dressing. Unfussy outfits like skirts with jumpers, and simple dresses with low-heeled shoes came into fashion. The focal point of a dress was its neckline, typically adorned with a Peter Pan collar, pussy-cat bow or ruffles. Soft, wide, flowing trousers were popular casual-wear items (they were called pyjamas until mid-decade and 'slacks' thereafter). They were worn mostly for entertaining and lounging at home or on the beach, rather than out on the street.

The austerity caused by the precarious state of the world economy sparked public health fears which led to a fitness craze. Inspired by the formation in Britain of the Women's League of Health & Beauty, women took up a range of leisure activities, including keep-fit, hiking and sunbathing. In 1936, the launch of Tampax enabled women to wear tighter, one-piece bathing costumes. These swimsuits could not be described as skimpy, but they were more revealing and allowed for greater freedom of movement than earlier bathing attire. The famous American tennis player Alice Marble outraged Wimbledon when she appeared on court in shorts. Nevertheless, women soon adopted shorts as leisurewear, along with straw hats, sunglasses and canvas pumps or espadrilles.

Sales of Butterick paper patterns soared as women sought to recreate the glamour of Paris and Hollywood on their home sewing machines. In 1933, Fred Astaire and Ginger Rogers made the hugely popular movie *Flying Down to Rio* and went on to complete at least one film a year for the rest of the decade. Among other things, these movies acted as a showcase for Ginger Rogers' gorgeous costumes. Hollywood, aided by technological and distribution

· 24 ·

THE INVENTIVE THIRTIES

American actress Betty Grable became *the* number one pin-up girl and was famed for her beautiful legs. The Hollywood studios took every opportunity to ensure that these assets were on display in a host of widely distributed 'cheesecake' publicity shots, such as this from 1937.

advances, became the flipside of the Threadbare Thirties, creating confections of costume with no apparent regard for cost. Designer Travis Banton regularly visited Paris, once buying up the city's entire stock of bugle beads and paillettes from under the aristocratic nose of Schiaparelli, presumably to use in one of his fabulous creations for Marlene Dietrich or Mae West at Paramount Pictures.

Hollywood costume designers had the task of creating high-fashion clothes for a film's release that, crucially, would still need to look fresh at the end of the run, which might be years later. Adrian (Adolph Greenberg) designed Madame Vionnet-inspired bias-cut satin gowns for Jean Harlow and was responsible for Joan Crawford's white organdie dress in *Letty Lynton*. This gown, with its large ruffled sleeves, was copied by Macy's and sold out all over the United States. The padded shoulders (designed to minimize Crawford's generous hips) would become a mainstay of Forties styling.

ABOVE Jean Patou's 1938 autumn collection featured an evening dress ('La Grande Robe de Tulle Noir') and a scarlet day outfit of fitted coat and hat.

OPPOSITE Ginger Rogers and Fred Astaire in characteristically glamorous evening attire in the film *Flying Down to Rio* (c.1933).

The revealing evening frocks of the Twenties were replaced by sophisticated gowns that covered more of the body, but revealed areas such as the back and shoulders (or a single shoulder in the asymmetric design). Backless evening dresses in sleek satins, with long strands of beads worn hanging down the backbone, were all the rage. There was a revival of classicism – dresses by Madame Grès and Augusta Bernard resembled the draperies of the Ancient Greeks. Lucien Lelong added a train and bustle to his lamé creations, Edward Molyneux incorporated a split skirt in some of his elegant designs and Schiaparelli favoured fantails for her slender gowns.

But high fashion still revolved around Vionnet's bias-cut dress, worn with elegant T-bar shoes.

Wallis Simpson was first mentioned in *Vogue* in 1935: 'the best-dressed women, like Mrs Ernest Simpson . . . have Schiaparelli's "pouch" dress in silk or printed cotton'. Wallis went on to marry the Duke of Windsor (himself a natty dresser), bringing international publicity to Mainbocher, who designed her pale-blue wedding dress. The Thirties were not so threadbare for the wealthy after all, and the populous looked on with envy. Finally, when cheap rayon resulted in widespread copying of the 'Wally' dress, the dominance of haute couture began to fade.

ABOVE Writer, heiress and political activist Nancy Cunard at the Grampian Hotel in Harlem in 1932, looking strikingly modern in a leather belted aviator-style jacket over a long black gabardine skirt. Known for her unconventional style, Cunard's passion for African artefacts is demonstrated here by her turban and trademark armful of heavy bangles.

OPPOSITE Edward Steichen's 1931 photo of two women in eveningwear. On the left, a black satin bias-cut evening dress with a white satin three-quarter-length bow-tied sleeved jacket by Lanvin. On the right, a Chanel chiffon gown with angel sleeves and plunging backline, accentuated by a jewel detail.

RIGHT This mid-to-late Thirties Italian hat of black polished fine straw has a slanted crown decorated with a grosgrain ribbon and artificial (probably silk) gardenias. It is unusual to find high hats in such mint condition because they did not fit easily into a standard hatbox.

PAGES 30 AND 31 This 1932 illustration for *Vogue* by Jean Pages shows (left to right) a Goupy blue linen and crochet suit with Chanel jersey beret; a Schiaparelli pink apron dress with pink enamel clasps at the back and a Descat hat; a yellow Jacquard weave piqué jacket by E'Ahetz; a striped linen shirt-fronted dress by Lyolène; a white linen dress with boat neck and deep V back by Vera Borea; a tweed coat with cape shoulders by Schiaparelli; and a tweed skirt with red broadcloth shirt by Chanel.

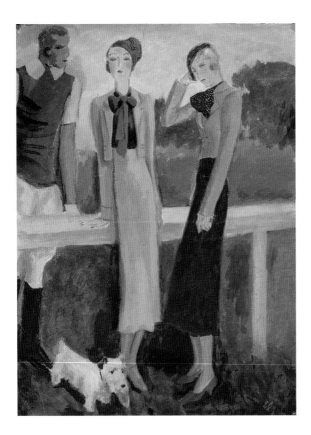

ABOVE A 1932 drawing by Edouard Garcia Benito shows two women at a polo match sporting Schiaparelli. The elegant, elongated skirts and pussy-cat bows are typical early Elsa; their Sicilian caps, worn askew, lend a hint of the exotic.

OPPOSITE Marlene Dietrich, at the height of her fame at Paramount Pictures in 1933, strides along the studio's Hollywood Street. She is dressed in an off-duty outfit of masculine-styled single-breasted suit with wide turned-up trousers worn with brogues, black turtleneck sweater, jaunty beret, white gloves and matching handkerchief. Dietrich was largely responsible for popularizing slacks as a glamorous but practical item of daywear for women.

THE ZIPPER

In 1851, Elias Howe, inventor of the sewing machine, received a patent for his 'automatic continuous clothing closure'. However, for some reason Howe did not go ahead with the marketing of his invention. In 1913, Gideon Sundback, a Swedish-born electrical engineer at the Universal Fastener Company, came up with a design for the modern zip. A patent for the 'separable fastener' was issued in 1917.

The name 'zipper' was coined by the B. F. Goodrich Company, where the fastener was used on a new type of rubber boot. It is thought that the name derived from the 'zipping' noise the fastener made when the boots were done up. For the next 20 years, the zip featured mainly on boots and tobacco pouches – no one appeared to entertain the idea of including it in garments. In the Thirties, a campaign to help children dress themselves saw the use of zippers in children's clothes, but it was not until zips became lighter and slimmer (with the invention of nylon in 1935) that they began to appear in women's clothing.

In 1933, the Lightning Fastener Company offered Elsa Schiaparelli $10,000 (about $100,000 today) to use their zips in her clothing. In her 1935–36 winter collection, Schiaparelli went one better and incorporated colourful plastic zips into her designs, exposing instead of concealing them. For the first time, zips appeared at necklines, in shoulder seams and on pockets and sleeves. The use of visible zips became synonymous with Schiaparelli and elevated the humble zipper to haute couture status.

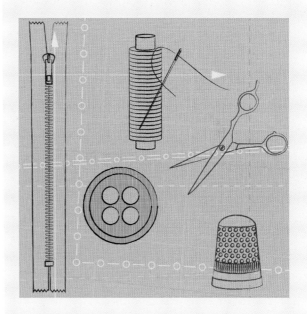

OPPOSITE This 1935 photograph by Horst P. Horst shows a woman modelling satin pyjamas designed for glamorous day lounging. They are worn under a Cossack-style button-through tunic with emperor sleeves and teamed with a favourite Thirties accessory – metallic leather T-bar sandals.

RIGHT Around 1935, a model wears a belted black wool and leopard-skin panelled dress under a matching coat with leopard-skin revers and large cuffs by Vionnet. The ensemble is accessorized with a black felt hat by Rose Descat and long gloves.

BELOW A classic Thirties clutch bag made of crocodile skin with a gilt and *pietra dura* acorn clasp. Clutch bags were typically envelope-shaped and larger for day than for evening, when they were designed to hold only a compact, lipstick and handkerchief.

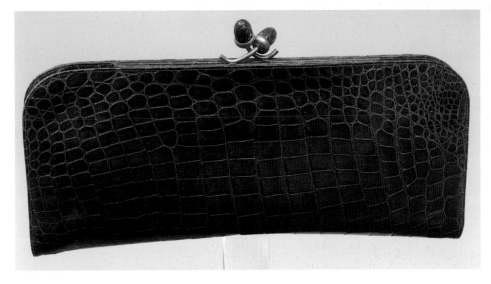

OPPOSITE This atmospheric shot demonstrates the influence of Hollywood lighting techniques on fashion photography. The model wears a Revillon astrakhan jacket with bell sleeves. The garment has a single self-covered button, slouch pockets and a corsage detail. Accessories include dark gloves, a clutch bag and a Lilly Daché polished straw 'Chinese' hat.

RIGHT Movie star Jean Harlow, the 'Blonde Bombshell', in one of her trademark bias-cut clingy satin gowns. This one, with draped cowl neckline and train, was designed by Adrian for the 1935 film *Reckless*.

BELOW Salvatore Ferregamo's scientific and creative approach to shoe design resulted in many innovations, including wedge and platform heels. He often incorporated unusual materials – these beautiful 1938 gold leather and red suede sandals with decorative stitching have covered cork heels.

LEFT A Salvador Dali-inspired 1936 Cecil Beaton photograph of women modelling Schiaparelli's spare elegant wool suits with long plain skirts. Simple hats, bag and gloves allow the surreal 'chest of drawers' pockets to dominate.

OPPOSITE A Horst P. Horst Hollywood-style shot of Coco Chanel in 1937 in which she models her own design, a three-quarter-length, single-breasted military-influenced wool coat with astrakhan trim, cuffs and shawl collar with arrowhead detail. The outfit is topped off with a costume metal-and-pearl brooch adorning a matching astrakhan hat.

PAGE 40 A 1937 *Vogue* photograph of a model wearing a Robert Piguet Grecian-style draped, pale (possibly oyster), heavy satin sleeveless evening gown. Christian Dior declared that 'Piguet taught me the virtues of simplicity through which true elegance must come'. The necklace by Ostertag emphasizes the low V neckline. The model's elaborate hairstyle is by Guillaume.

PAGE 41 Socialite, fashion editor and style icon Barbara 'Babe' Paley (declared 'Super-Dresser of Our Time' by *Vanity Fair* in 1974) photographed in the late Thirties dressed to kill in a Marten fur jacket with jabot revers. The hat, by John Frederics, is decorated with fur and bird plumage.

The Frugal Forties

Chanel left Paris in 1939 declaring, 'I thought there wouldn't be any more dresses', but fashion kept calm and carried on. The Paris shows of January 1940, just months before the German occupation, showed understandably restrained collections. Only Schiaparelli anticipated the 'New Look' by elongating the boxy shoulders of dresses and jackets; then she, like Chanel, Vionnet and many other designers, left town. One who stayed, Jeanne Lanvin, gave her designs names like 'Free France'; another, Madame Grès, produced patriotic dresses in red, white and blue. With Europe plunged into war, New York sought to take advantage by becoming the centre of international fashion. However, as Schiaparelli put it, 'the Eiffel Tower is not displaced by the Empire State Building'. Nevertheless, Claire McCardell emerged as a homegrown quality designer whose timeless 'American' styles are collectors' pieces today. In San Francisco, Adolph Schuman charted a rags-to-riches rise to success with his 'Lilli Ann' brand of top-quality glamorously trimmed tailoring.

Back in Britain, the government introduced rationing and 'utility' or CC41 (Controlled Commodity 1941) clothing in 1942, along with price controls and strict limits on the number of designs and the amount of fabric and buttons used per garment. 'Austerity' directives meant that the number of pockets and pleats was limited and braid was banned. Zips, turn-ups and lace were not allowed either, but the government managed to produce desirable good-quality clothing by commissioning top-class designers like Hartnell and Bianca Mosca.

The fashion staple remained the knee-length skirt or dress teamed with a long, square-shouldered jacket, often patterned. The 'make do and mend' concept was embraced as women ran up skirts from coupon-free black-out fabric and slips from parachute silk. Shoes were sturdy with low or wedge heels. All new clothing, including stockings, was restricted by rationing, so women painted seams down the backs of their legs or wore trousers outside work to preserve their precious supply of hosiery. When it became important to carry a gas mask outdoors at all times, women discovered the convenience of shoulder bags.

With many women engaged in war work, the snood or turban (popularized by Winston Churchill's wife Clementine) became the usual headgear, as it was handy for covering unwashed locks and preventing long hair from becoming tangled in machinery. Trousers were donned by land girls and factory workers, who also often wore a scarf knotted on top of the head. After work, these women recycled second-hand clothing (exempt from the rationing rules) or turned pre-war clothes into new ones (scarves into a skirt, for example, in a *Vogue* issue of 1943).

Patriotic images were printed on rayon handbags and scarves in the UK. In the United States, military-influenced fashion appeared (the Eisenhower-style waist-length jacket was particularly popular) and American girls with sweethearts in the forces wore US insignia as brooches. In Paris, Lelong designed a charm bracelet of miniature jeeps.

In 1941, when the United States entered the Second World War, Hollywood lent its support with a raft of morale-boosting films. Going to the movies was a cheap form of enjoyment and escapism and cinemagoers became so engrossed that they frequently ignored the air-raid warnings that flashed across the screen. Hollywood costume designers were allowed luxury materials to make show-stopping

The influence of the young Lauren Bacall is evident in the styling of this
model for a Horst P. Horst 1947 fashion shot. Bacall emerged as a leading
lady alongside Humphrey Bogart in the film *To Have and Have Not* (1944).
In this photograph, a marl-grey cap-sleeved side-buttoned tunic
is worn with a matching skirt with draping detail and gold bracelets.

dresses, such as Jean Louis' famous sumptuous satin strapless gown for Rita Hayworth in *Gilda*. Joan Crawford worked her wide shoulders again in her Oscar-winning comeback *Mildred Pierce*, a look that was readily taken up by wartime fashion followers because shoulder pads were easily made from rags and were a cheap way to update old clothes. Trousers appeared on the front cover of *Vogue* for the first time in the Forties, their popularity enhanced by press coverage of Marlene Dietrich and Katharine Hepburn striding around the movie set in slacks.

When Paris was liberated in 1944, the city's fashion industry scrambled to regain its status as couture capital of the world. Long hemlines, full skirts and extravagant evening gowns appeared in the 1945 Paris collections, but were not bought by the export market. Restrictions were still in place in the UK and USA. Also, Paris' fashion reputation had been tainted as some members of the industry, who had designed opulent garments for Germans during the war, were accused of collusion. It took a portly man with a genius for timing (and an arrangement with the textile magnate Marcel Boussac) to reclaim the fashion capital crown for the French.

In 1947, Christian Dior launched his 'Corolla' line (dubbed the 'New Look' by *Harper's Bazaar* editor Carmel Snow) to 'liberate all women from a poverty-stricken era'. Some outfits required up to 45 metres of fabric (15 times the allowance for a typical British wartime dress) in order to create the long voluptuous skirt bolstered with layer upon layer of petticoats. Sloping shoulders and a tiny waist, which appeared even smaller when contrasted with the generously padded hips, defined this ultra-feminine shape. After a decade of frugal living, this was the look women had been waiting for and it became an immediate sensation. Within months, the New Look had swept through the entire fashion industry to become the dominant silhouette of the Fifties.

Actress Loretta Young poses in a simple white short-sleeved trouser suit in 1941. The wide-legged pants are balanced by clumpy white platform shoes.

Rita Hayworth became a major Hollywood star during the Forties. Her erotic appeal as a *femme fatale* was best captured in the film *Gilda* (1946), in which she performed a legendary one-glove striptease while wearing a sleek strapless black gown designed by Jean Louis.

Look pretty ... *Have fun*

A washable cotton that will fit into your budget with ease.

A lovable frock skirted with a flaring charm.

STYLE 1300
Sizes 9 - 17
Value Priced
$5.98

Fabric: "Pandora Broadcloth" (Cotton)

Fashion Frocks

ABOVE A plate from an early Forties clothing catalogue, complete with fabric samples. Catalogues were sent to retailers to enable them to select their seasonal collection. This washable cotton 'Fashion Frocks' dress was aimed at the younger budget-conscious consumer. White gloves and pearls were worn by every generation of women at this time.

LEFT A 1940 Horst P. Horst photograph of a model in a buttercup-yellow rayon playsuit consisting of ruched-front swimsuit with shoelace straps under matching shorts. The look is pulled together with early plastic sunglasses and fabric espadrilles with wedge heels and black ankle-tie ribbons.

OPPOSITE An early Forties magazine publicity shot showing an autumn/winter range of sturdy but stylish leather shoes and toning gauntlet-length day gloves. The model wears a burnt-khaki coloured jacket with dove-grey hat over a black crocheted snood. Make-up consists of ultra-fashionable matte red lipstick and matching nail polish.

LEFT Movie actress Janis Paige wearing a mocha-coloured wool day suit by Milo Anderson, Warner Brothers' costume designer. The outfit consists of a pencil skirt with front slit, a jacket with padded shoulders and spaghetti-waist-tie fastening. It is teamed with a veiled and feathered black hat, suede gloves, matching bag and typical Forties sandals with ankle straps and peep toes.

ABOVE An advertisement published in *Harper's Bazaar* in 1940 exhorts readers to 'Plan for the Duration: Invest in Quality' – the motto of British retailer Jaeger during the war years. The sketches show a camel-hair trenchcoat, a dress and a housecoat designed along similar lines to the utility range which was about to be launched at this point. Jaeger also published 'Essentials for the Forces' knitting patterns.

OPPOSITE The 'Pocket Venus', Veronica Lake was a major sex symbol of the Forties, famed for her alluring and much-imitated peek-a-boo hairstyle. This free-flowing look was eventually banned in munitions factories during the war years after female workers got their hair caught in machinery. For Lake's wardrobe in *I Married a Witch* (1942), Edith Head and her fellow costume designers were allowed to use acres of extravagant fabric to enhance the actress's glamour and help boost public morale. This black chiffon over nude silk evening dress with Guipre lace bodice detail and bishop sleeves is a perfect foil for Lake's smouldering beauty.

LEFT A publicity photograph taken at the Board of Trade in London in 1942 shows models wearing the new utility fashions. Britain's top designers were asked to create a collection that focused on style and cut. Wartime austerity measures dictated that skirts were allowed only two box or four knife pleats and had to be a regulation 18 inches (46 cm) above the ground. This tailored style became the standard silhouette of the war years.

OPPOSITE A 1941 John Rawlings photograph of a model in a broad-striped turquoise and tulip-red moiré taffeta summer evening dress with wide, slightly puffed shoulders, short sleeves and belted waist with bow. This stunning gown is teamed with red satin sandals and toning ruched evening gloves.

HOORAY FOR HOLLYWOOD!

During the war years, most of the jobs undertaken by women involved tough physical work in unpleasant conditions. Inexpensive regular trips to the cinema were a welcome relief from everyday hardship. Women's workwear was usually dungarees or adapted menswear, with hair scraped back beneath a turban, so any glamour, even borrowed for a couple of hours, was a huge luxury. Film costume designers were urged to boost public morale. To achieve this, they were given large budgets and were exempt from wartime clothing restrictions.

Films blending romance and patriotism were extremely popular. For *Casablanca* (1942), Ingrid Bergman's glamorous gowns were designed by Australian-born Orry-Kelly. For *Now, Voyager* (1942) Bette Davis' sleek fitted costumes with stunning diamond brooches and iconic veiled hat were created by Edith Head, a favourite designer among many female stars.

Occasionally, as evidenced by the romantic comedies *Cover Girl* and *Pin Up Girl* (both 1944), the movie's plot wasn't as important as the spectacle of its stars clad in lavish costumes and immortalized in glorious Technicolor. Women's magazines carried tips on how to rework the Hollywood look at home, using 'make do and mend' techniques. Even *Vogue* fell into line with the austerity message, decreeing that 'anything elaborate looks silly.'

ABOVE A 1943 propaganda-posing-as-fashion photograph encourages the purchase of war bonds. The model is dressed for work in a crisp cotton candy-striped pinafore over a cuff-sleeved blouse. A snood covers her hair and she wears no jewellery (ostentatious jewellery was considered vulgar during the war years).

OPPOSITE A 1943 *Vogue* plate of a model in a Henri Bendel ensemble, consisting of a flame-red cellophane-straw hat with black cigarette band, matching skirt and matinée-length gloves. A black pussy-cat bow scarf is worn over a white blouse with a high collar, dress shirt plastron and leg-o'-mutton sleeves. Note the perfectly matching lipstick!

THE FRUGAL FORTIES

ABOVE Dior's sensational 'New Look' in 1947 sent shockwaves through the fashion establishment. Its padded sloping shoulders and hips, tiny waist and very full mid-calf-length skirt were in direct contrast to the tailoring that had gone before. Women the world over immediately embraced the extravagant feminine style as an antidote to the straitened war years.

OPPOSITE Around 1946, a model in a Ceil Chapman (reportedly Marilyn Monroe's favourite designer) coat of navy Farnsworth wool tweed, with covered buttons and a stand-up collar, over a navy skirt. She carries the coat's curly lamb detachable lining as a travel rug.

RIGHT Actress and icon Katharine Hepburn in her stateroom on board the SS *Nieuw Amsterdam* in 1948, wearing slacks with a white turtleneck under a linen overshirt, teamed with American loafers. Off set, Hepburn tended to favour a masculine look. With her spirited personality and East Coast breeding, she was universally considered a 'class act' and helped to make the wearing of trousers acceptable for women.

ABOVE Mme Jeanine Decaux at the 'Grande Semaine' car show in Paris in 1949, wearing a Nina Ricci black-and-white polka dot, V-necked, belted, mid-calf full-skirted dress. The cuffed three-quarter-length sleeves add to the air of casual elegance, as do the day gloves, ankle-tied two-tone mid-heel sandals and wide-brimmed hat trimmed with ostrich fronds. The car is apparently a 20 HP Delahaye – but who cares?!

LEFT A 1949 fashion photo, taken two years after the launch of the New Look. The image shows Dior's abiding influence in the dove-grey flannel suit with a cinched waist and long knife-pleated skirt. Subtle colour is added by way of a red beret worn on the side of the head together with cream kid gloves and matching umbrella.

OPPOSITE A model poses in front of the Bernard Lamotte mural in the French National Tourist Office in New York, 1949. She wears a day costume of self-striped moiré taffeta mandarin-collared blouse with large fretwork lace Puritan cuffs and a long dark skirt with a cinched waist. The outfit is by Jacques Fath for Joseph Halpert; the pearl necklace worn as a bracelet is by Karu.

The Ultra-Feminine Fifties

For many people, the start of the Fifties felt like a new beginning after the war. There was an air of optimism, bolstered in the UK by the influential Festival of Britain in London in 1951. Work was plentiful, so young people, particularly if they lived at home as most of them did, had a regular disposable income to spend at the 'flicks' and on a lifestyle and clothes influenced by the movies. With her demure dresses and sorbet-coloured knits, American actress and singer Doris Day epitomized the fashionable girl-next-door type and was hugely popular on both sides of the Atlantic. For her role in *Sabrina* in 1954, the gamine Audrey Hepburn was dressed in haute couture by Givenchy and became, with Grace Kelly, the ideal of the elegant Fifties female.

After the war, many women left work and returned to the home to become full-time housewives. With the New Look's full-skirted influence, there was a return to a more 'feminine' wardrobe of printed cotton frocks often in floral, check, polka dot or novelty patterns to give a fun feeling. Circle skirts in sequinned cotton or in felt with appliquéd designs (the poodle being a favourite) were worn with pastel twinsets (beaded for evening wear) and stiletto heels to give an ultra-feminine shape.

Handbags, especially in America, were also being designed with whimsy in mind. Stylecraft of Miami specialized in novelty purses, including shaped straw baskets incorporating gold-flecked vinyl and box bags with 'stardust, pearl and shell finishes'. These, together with Lucite purses by companies such as Wilardy and Maxim, are highly collectable today and still eminently usable.

Claire McCardell retained her position as the USA's favourite designer with her relaxed, easy-to-wear 'American Look' of simple shapes in cotton gingham or denim with clever detailing. Her 'popover' wrap dress was a forerunner of Diane von Fürstenberg's trademark garment. Meanwhile, Bonnie Cashin concentrated on ready-to-wear (sportswear) separates that could be mixed and matched in a very modern way.

In Britain, the utility scheme ended in 1952 and crisp cotton summer dresses with full skirts, slim belts and, typically, matching boleros were popular with all ages. Younger women also wore waffle or piqué playsuits consisting of matching shorts, top and skirt. Horrockses' top-quality cotton dresses were the subject of stylish adverts shot by John French. Other British manufacturers enjoying success included Sambo, Blanes and Alice Edwards. A vital component of the full Fifties silhouette was the new nylon petticoat, which was easy to wash and wear and kept its shape without support.

In 1954, in an ambitious move, Chanel, now aged 70, launched her comeback collection. Despite claims by sceptics that it was merely a reprise of her glory days, Chanel would become the most important designer in the world during this decade. Her innovations in the Fifties included gold chains, gilt and pearl earrings, Breton fashions, shoes with contrasting toe-caps and much more besides.

OPPOSITE All that heaven allows: a 1955 photograph of a model wearing a broad-striped button-through dress with fitted bodice, sash belt and full skirt. The (almost) matching straw carrier gives the look a lighthearted, quirky feel typical of much Fifties styling.

French actress and model Brigitte Bardot on the set of *La Lumière d'en face* (1955). Bardot's sex symbol status endured into the Sixties. Here her gamine sensuality is enhanced by a breathlessly figure-hugging aluminium-grey dress.

In February 1955, Chanel launched the 2.55 bag, its iconic diamond quilting said to have been inspired by the windows of the orphanage in which she grew up. The 2.55 is still the most instantly recognizable handbag of all time.

For eveningwear, ballgowns with New Look proportions were fashionable. This was an understandable reaction to the previous years, when lavish gowns (even if they had been bought pre-war) were frowned upon and often remodelled into less ostentatious garments. Halterneck evening dresses were particularly popular after Marilyn Monroe sported the ivory-coloured, pleated Travilla dress in *The Seven Year Itch* (1955).

The release of the pop song 'Rock Around the Clock' (and the film of the same name in 1956) coincided with a generation of wartime baby boomers becoming teenagers and led to the cultural explosion of rock and roll. Girls wanted clothes they could dance in; many favoured circle skirts worn

Marilyn Monroe wearing William Travilla's ivory cocktail dress in the subway grille scene from *The Seven Year Itch* – one of the most iconic images of the twentieth century.

with layers of net petticoat and cinched at the waist with a belt. Skirts or jeans were teamed with a blouse and cardigan (with the latter often simply worn over the shoulders), flat shoes and ankle-length 'bobby' socks. Rockabilly girls favoured cropped jeans, crisp blouses, cardigans with the sleeves rolled up and scarves tied kerchief-style around the neck.

Actress Lana Turner, the 'sweater girl', single-handedly revitalized the image of knitwear which overnight went from frumpy to fashionable. Most women filled in the V at the neck with a scarf or rows of pearls. In haute couture, Dior had been amending the New Look silhouette on an annual basis. However, his dominance took a knock in 1957, when Basque designer Cristóbal Balenciaga launched a simple garment with an undefined waist, which became known as the sack dress.

By the end of the decade, the silicon chip had been patented and Sputnik 1 launched into the great unknown. The Sixties were about to begin.

ABOVE Singer and dancer Josephine Baker photographed aboard the French Line's SS *Liberté* as the ship arrived in New York harbour on 3 October 1950. Famous for her near nude performances a couple of decades earlier, Miss Baker sported a chic ensemble of tailored double-breasted jacket of fine wool with a slight slub effect, a black handbag with a stylish perpendicular strap and a matching hat with tassel.

LEFT This 1952 'sports ensemble' consists of a mandarin-collared sleeveless blouse made of silk surah, patterned with tiny beige-and-white checks. The blouse has a bodice front and oval, mother-of-pearl buttons. It is worn over silk shantung pedal pushers with very large patch pockets and an attached tabbed belt fastening at the back. The outfit was designed by Claire McCardell (creator of the 'American Look') for Townley.

OPPOSITE Balenciaga's 1952 poppy-red linen suit of a slim skirt under a boxy jacket with slight trapeze swing to the back and sleeves. A buttoned tab detail accentuates the waist. The suit is worn with white, pushed-down gloves, a tiny red straw boater and toning lipstick.

ABOVE American model Sunny Hartnett in 1953, wearing Irish designer Digby Morton's camel-hair and wool suit as part of a single colour ensemble. The elongated, narrow-belted dress has a stand-up neckline; the swing jacket and dress have corresponding pocket details. The day hat is by Knox, the leather bag with metal handle is by Milch, the walnut earrings are by Coro, the 'Vivid' lipstick is by Yardley and the car is by Rolls-Royce.

OPPOSITE Early supermodel Suzy Parker in Givenchy's 1953 jet-black quilted satin jacket with opera-length sleeves, worn over a gloriously full rose-pink Chinese lacquer printed skirt with knife pleats. Black net petticoats lend further fullness and pixie-toed black high-heeled day pumps complete the look.

ABOVE Actress and style icon Audrey Hepburn on the set of *Sabrina* (1954) directed by Billy Wilder and costumed by Edith Head, who won an Oscar for her work. Hepburn's red felt Peter Pan-collared blouse with appliquéd poodle was designed for the ingénue section of the film, as poodles were a very fashionable motif in teenage wear of the mid-Fifties.

LEFT A 1952 Schiaparelli evening dress of navy-blue taffeta with a three-point bodice. The skirt has Venus de Milo drapery and a bustle of azalea-red paper taffeta. The refined look is finished off with opera-length evening gloves and simple earrings.

OPPOSITE Celebrated fashion photographer Henry Clarke's 1954 shot of a model in a Jacques Fath evening gown of rose-printed, satin-striped silk organdie with a collared neckline and tight bodice, fuchsia-pink satin accordion-pleated belt and sweeping skirt.

PLASTIC FANTASTIC!

In 1927, when the patents on Bakelite expired, synthetic coloured plastic became a material of choice in the United States. This was particularly true in the Fifties, when post-war America aspired to all things 'modern'. Companies like Wilardy Originals and Charles S. Kahn competed to make the most innovative and unusual plastic handbags. Although these were relatively expensive, they were embraced by women of all ages for their fashion and novelty value.

Another new plastic, called 'acetate', was used for handbags – and clothes, too. It especially suited Fifties garments that called for pleats or draping. Acetate rayon was stronger than viscose rayon, but still very easy to wash and popular for daywear. Acetate could also be made into synthetic chiffon and satin for affordable, figure-hugging gowns.

ABOVE Model Anne St Marie wears Chanel's long red wool pencil skirt under a leopard-print shirt-jacket with buttoned cuffs. This photograph was taken a year after Chanel's triumphant 1954 comeback and the same year in which she launched the iconic quilted handbag.

OPPOSITE TOP Grace Kelly, the quintessential aloof, icy blonde and face of the Fifties in Alfred Hitchcock's *Rear Window* (1954) – with James Stewart looking on. Kelly's ensemble, designed by Edith Head, is a typical Fifties suit of long straight skirt and soft jacket in mint-green linen with a draped silk blouse. Pushed-up sleeves and pushed-down gloves were very fashionable during the decade.

OPPOSITE BOTTOM A 1954 acetate white jersey evening dress by Paquin; the gown is criss-crossed from the décolletage to just above the knee, then flares into a mermaid flounce. It is worn with an acetate satin cape in French blue with a scarlet lining.

ABOVE Pierre Balmain once said that 'dressmaking is the architecture of movement', a commitment to elegance borne out by this 1955 ensemble. The elongated pencil skirt is made of self-striped suiting wool; it buttons at the back and has tabbed pockets on the hip. It is worn with a sealskin slipover hooded cape. The slender silhouette is further defined by opera-length gloves and an oversized clutch bag.

OPPOSITE Dior's 'A line' collection launched in 1955 and included this lightweight tartan wool jacketed dress. The effect of the A line was to flatten the bosom and square the waist. This version, with narrow sleeves and a pleated classic-length skirt, is worn with elbow-length gloves, a petal hat and high pumps with Mary Jane straps.

LEFT It's 1957, and Hollywood star Ava Gardner models clothes made for her by the Fontana Sisters in Rome. This black taffeta sheath is decorated with a tiered panel of Spanish lace attached with a red rose above the hip and accessorized with black satin cocktail shoes and a veil hairpiece.

OPPOSITE A late Fifties jonquil-yellow suit made from *Vogue* pattern S-4867. The boxy tapered jacket with black buttons and three-quarter-length sleeves is worn over a long slim pencil skirt. The pale suit contrasts dramatically with black patent leather stilettos and handbag and a black-and-white silk scarf worn as a turban. *Vogue* paper patterns were more expensive than other brands, but they provided a relatively cheap template that women could follow to make their own designer clothes.

THE ULTRA-FEMININE FIFTIES

LEFT American 'sportswear' designer Bonnie Cashin reintroduced the tunic to fashion. This 1958 photograph shows a black-and-forest-green windowpane mohair plaid pullover with leather binding. The tunic is teamed with leather cigarette pants and flat ankle-skimming suede boots by Fortunet.

OPPOSITE This image shows two styles forever associated with the Fifties: the 'sweater' look popularized by Lana Turner (aided by the advent of the conical bra) and the felt circle skirt with novelty feature. Here, an appliquéd beaded umbrella doubles as a pocket.

The Psychedelic Sixties

The Sixties was the decade in which the pendulum of fashion swung firmly towards London. The revered editor of American *Vogue* Diana Vreeland confirmed this by dedicating a 1964 issue to the 'British Invasion'. In 1955, in an era when 'fashion wasn't designed for young people', Mary Quant had opened a boutique on the King's Road in Chelsea. She found herself on the right street at the right time and became one of the best-known faces of the 'youthquake' that erupted during London's Swinging Sixties. The miniskirt was the iconic garment of the decade and debate still rages over who invented it. While André Courrèges was the first couturier to raise hemlines to mid-thigh in his futuristic 'Space Age' collection of 1964, it was undeniably Quant who popularized the mini. With her trademark Vidal Sassoon bob, Quant *was* her own brand. Her PVC go-go boots, acid-coloured tights and Pop Art dresses epitomized the era.

The Sixties revolutionized dressing for the young, with a new focus on individualism and being 'with-it'. It wasn't just love that became free. Hair that had been tortured into backcombed bouffant styles was shorn or left loose. Girls (and boys) wore clashing combinations, jeans and T-shirts, ethnic kaftans, fake leopard-skin, ex-army clobber, their granny's fur coats and anything else that took their fancy.

Haute couture began to look to the street for inspiration. Models from 'ordinary' rather than aristocratic backgrounds emerged, such as Jean 'the Shrimp' Shrimpton and the teenage Twiggy, whose huge waif-like eyes and natural androgyny became the essence of 'mod cool'. Pop groups such as the Rolling Stones, with their tight hipster trousers, and the Beatles (their sharp mod-style suits to be replaced by fancy dress uniforms as the decade wore on) reinforced the fashion/music symbiosis that was key to youth identity. For the first time, fashion was dictated by the young, many of whom suddenly felt empowered. Increased wealth and social mobility, advances in birth control, new ideas springing from feminism, interest in the space race and improvements in manmade fabrics all fed into the fashion revolution.

Although Quant claimed that in her boutique 'you will find a duchess jostling with a typist to buy the same dresses', her clothes were too expensive for most young women. In 1964, Barbara Hulanicki came up with a more cost-effective solution when she opened the first Biba in a former chemist's shop in Kensington. Flying in the face of modernity, Biba went for a dimly-lit period feel; floppy hats, Deco-print tea dresses, feather boas and smoky-coloured satin vamp blouses with leg-o'-mutton sleeves were displayed on bentwood hatstands. Equally significant was the work of designer Jean Muir who engineered jersey, silk and crêpe in muted colours and designs so timeless that they look new today.

For the first time, London influenced Paris fashions. Paco Rabanne built on Courrèges' space-age designs, producing sculptural minidresses forged from chainmail, scrap metal and plastic; these were

OPPOSITE In New York City, 1965, five models wear Pierre Cardin dresses in the acid rainbow colours of the Sixties.

ABOVE In 1969, the retro Deco glamour of Biba is on display in this black-and-silver chevron-striped sequinned maxidress with matching headdress and black net veil.

OPPOSITE Actress Jane Fonda in a publicity portrait for the science fiction film *Barbarella* (1968). In her role as the eponymous 41st-century astronaut heroine, Fonda was directed by her husband Roger Vadim. Paco Rabanne designed her space-age costume.

often worn with lurex tights to complete the futuristic look. Perhaps because of his extreme youth, Yves Saint Laurent was able to straddle the past, present and future with his Mondrian-inspired block colour tunic dresses. His 'le smoking' women's tuxedo heralded the acceptance of trousers – specifically as eveningwear – for smart women, but it was Pierre Cardin who most innovatively combined futuristic ideas with couture cutting techniques to produce the thoroughly modern tubular and moulded dresses.

Not everyone in fashion was designing for the Brave New World. Barbara Hulanicki repackaged the glamour of the Twenties and Thirties for Biba 'dolly birds'. The party of the decade, Truman Capote's 'Black-and-White Ball' of 1967, featured a dress code inspired by Cecil Beaton's sumptuous costumes for the musical *My Fair Lady* set in Edwardian London. In line with this retro theme, Laura Ashley struck a pastoral note with romantic dresses in fine cottons and nostalgic sprig prints with billowing sleeves, tiered skirts and high necklines.

However, in Italy, Emilio Pucci honed a distinctly Sixties style inspired by underground psychedelia. This he translated into whimsical haute couture, producing dramatic costumes of swirly-patterned wrinkle-free silk. Back in Britain, Ossie Clark was designing deceptively simple, flowing dresses in fresh, feminine Celia Birtwell prints. Meanwhile, teenagers unable to afford Zandra Rhodes' bohemian works of art used acid colours to tie-dye their own cheesecloth skirts and shirts.

Once skirts had risen as far as the micromini they could rise no further and it was inevitable that hemlines would drop again, to the relief of Britain's textile industry. Minis were superseded by the short-lived midi, then the maxi – a skirt length embraced equally by the burgeoning hippie generation and the bright young things of Carnaby Street. By the turn of the decade, flower power was 'in' and, as the 1969 Thunderclap Newman song presciently declared, there was 'Something in the Air' – though what that something was would turn out to be more complex and fragmented than many people envisaged.

ABOVE Susan Small designs for a London fashion show in 1960: the model on the left wears a Chantilly lace cocktail dress with long transparent sleeves and a wide V-neck; the model on the right sports a satin strapless dress with a petal skirt. Susan Small was a popular British label for party dresses designed initially for the petite market.

LEFT American conservative early-Sixties fashion demonstrates that it still has its heart in the Fifties. From left to right, a pale pink linen suit with knee-length pleated skirt; a sleeveless red-and-white geometric knit shift top with a navy wool skirt; and a camel-and-beige fine striped wool tweed coat.

OPPOSITE A 1961 photograph of a model wearing a fire-engine-red two-piece outfit of straight (though wider than the Fifties) pencil skirt and shift top, designed by Kimberley. The alligator pumps are by I. Miller, the handbag by Walter Katten and the beret by Emme Boutique. The photo was taken in Paris by Frances McLaughlin-Gill, the first female photographer to be awarded a contract with *Vogue*.

ABOVE Audrey Hepburn's popularity continued undimmed into the Sixties: in this 1964 photograph she models a puffed zebra-print beret. Hepburn's name is synonymous with that of Hubert de Givenchy, despite the fact that when the fashion designer first met her he believed he had an appointment with the then far-more-famous Hepburn – Katharine!

LEFT Models Sara Crichton-Stuart and Twiggy at the entrance of London's Hung On You boutique. Sara wears a navy-blue above-the-knee coat with a red/blue/yellow striped collar and Twiggy is modelling the matching dress, both by Daniel Hechter. The shoes are in fashionable two-tone primary colours.

OPPOSITE Dresses became shorter and showed more of a space age influence as the decade progressed. This shift dress is constructed out of black-, white- and coral-coloured paillettes over a nude bodysuit. The model's hair is shaped into an asymmetric bob, accentuated by a single black-and-white Pop Art earring.

OP ART

The Sixties saw a new generation of young women who no longer wanted, or had, to dress in 'junior miss' versions of their mothers' clothes. The mod explosion, which began in London, reflected an obsession with the future. The stark geometry of Op Art fashions meshed with the bold, simple silhouettes of A-line and shift dresses to create what Mary Quant called 'absolutely twentieth century fashion'.

The popularity of mod fashions in the USA coincided with a ground-breaking art exhibition in New York. 'The Responsive Eye' featured the Op Art work of British artist Bridget Riley. Her designs were widely reproduced on dresses in what Riley described as 'vulgarization by the rag trade'.

1966 beachwear by Gayle Kirkpatrick for Atelier includes a black-and-white Op Art bandeau top connected to an orange miniskirt (left), and a tank dress of fuchsia top and sunshine-yellow skirt with a white bull's eye on the chest. Both models wear wraparound visors by Halston.

ABOVE Saturday girls at Biba, London, in 1966 wear matching hooped-print minidresses with striped canvas belts. Note the suede go-go boots on the right. The Biba store's nostalgic formula of bentwood hatstands, vintage furniture and feather boas, together with the fashionable shop girls, would endure and be transferred to Big Biba during the next decade.

OPPOSITE In 1965, at the height of her fame, Jean Shrimpton models a vermilion suede cardigan-jacket with a box-pleat 'schoolgirl' skirt by Viola Sylbert for Highlander Sportswear. It is teamed with opaque white tights and black patent leather flats. The black straw hat (just visible) is by Emme Boutique.

LEFT Sex symbol Britt Ekland, photographed in 1967, wearing a black crêpe Jean Muir 'wrapper coat' trimmed with ostrich feathers and accessorized with black lace tights and a chunky ring.

OPPOSITE A model wears a 1965 Pierre Cardin beaded tubular minidress with cut-out shoulders in a striking Pop Art design of black 'bubbles' on a shocking pink background. Cardin was the designer who most successfully translated space age concepts into fashionwear.

BELOW A cropped sleeveless top and matching slimfit trousers with a slight flare in daisy cut-out fabric, designed by Jules-François Crahay for Lanvin's 1967 collection. The outfit is further defined by white patch pockets, gloves and flat 'sports' shoes.

OPPOSITE The late Sixties witnessed the explosion of psychedelia, with the Beatles' *Sergeant Pepper* album, experiments with psychedelic drugs and a growth in political awareness. Fashion mirrored this trend with bold, colourful fabrics and designs, as demonstrated by these three swirled minidresses from 1966. Left to right: a long-sleeved shift; a dress with sports collar and puffed cuffs; and a short-sleeved shift with matching neon orange plastic bangle. All dresses are made from silk chiffon and designed by Marc Bohan for Dior.

RIGHT Another outfit inspired by psychedelia: a bold-coloured geometric print jumpsuit with palazzo flares and a bodice with spaghetti straps, designed by Frank Smith for Saks Fifth Avenue. The white floppy sunhat is by Madcaps.

LEFT In 1967, designer Mary Quant demonstrates the look she became famous for with her Vidal Sassoon bobbed hair, minidress and low-heeled, knee-high boots. Quant's name and personal style were a brand that became synonymous with the Swinging Sixties.

OPPOSITE Emilio Pucci, the 'Prince of Prints', became world famous for his geometric designs in a kaleidoscope of colours. This 1967 Pucci sea-blue tile-patterned floating chiffon voile coat has an empire-line tie fastening. It is worn over a matching bodysuit.

BELOW André Courrèges studied engineering before transferring to fashion design. He introduced the miniskirt to France and, in 1964, launched his influential 'Space Age' collection, which used primary and metallic colours to great effect. This 1969 white sateen jumpsuit is decorated with white furry pompoms, brass discs and breast cups, all of which contrast dramatically with the model's red Dutch boy wig.

PAGES 92-93 In 1967, fashion model and party girl Penelope Tree wears a Paco Rabanne 'phosphorescent' dress made of neon-coloured plastic cut-out links over a black sheath. The 'stalagmite' headdress is by Alexandre Boutique.

The Riotous Seventies

Of all the dramatically different styles of clothing floating around at the end of the Sixties, seemingly the most unlikely – the ethnic peasant look beloved of hippies – made it into the 1970 Paris collections. This trend was echoed on Britain's streets, with shaggy Afghan fur coats seen everywhere over hot pants, kaftans or long floral frocks. Towards the end of the Sixties, movie-inspired vintage fashions started to take off. *Bonnie and Clyde* (1967) sparked a trend for Thirties-style knee-length A-line skirts worn with berets. Similarly, *The Boy Friend* (1971), *Cabaret* (1972) and *The Great Gatsby* (1974) all fuelled the craze for a glamorous Twenties look.

In 1973, Barbara Hulanicki moved Biba to the Art Deco Derry & Toms building in Kensington to create 'the most beautiful store in the world'. Floor upon floor of fantastical set-dressing showcased the glamorous merchandise; this included Forties-influenced black jersey outfits trimmed in mock ocelot, Thirties-style crêpe dresses with slingback shoes, and lurex brocade jackets with matching pillbox hats. Vintage (then simply known as second-hand) clothing was bought from markets, jumble sales and army surplus stores, although Miss Mouse (designed by Rae Spencer-Cullen) made cute retro-inspired novelty print clothes that sold in Topshop.

The decade enjoyed a riot of contrasting fashions. The short-lived 'glam rock' sensation was inspired by pop stars such as Marc Bolan and David Bowie, who wore tight 'feminine' (or sometimes women's) clothes, glitter and make-up. The platform boots and flares from this look remain shorthand for the Seventies today. The boots were Forties-influenced, but had towering platform soles and chunky heels. Flares were updated versions of Oxford bags, but dandified through the use of embroidered cotton or crushed velvet in jewel colours.

By contrast, a more casual form of dress became fashionable and designers began to focus on producing classic ready-to-wear lines. Jean Muir's timeless jersey separates and Yves Saint Laurent's tailored suits were very successful in Europe. Meanwhile, in the United States, Ralph Lauren and Calvin Klein led the market in chic informal classics and with the new 'sportswear as daywear' look epitomized by Geoffrey Beene's designs.

In 1977, *Saturday Night Fever* burst onto cinema screens. Before long, glowing white suits inspired by the film were being aired in the new discos and at New York's Studio 54 nightclub. Even if you couldn't afford Halston, Gucci or Fiorucci, the disco was the place to dress up and anything went as long as it was loud and trashy. Typical disco outfits included bold-coloured bodysuits made of Spandex with contrasting belts and matching high heels, or off-the-shoulder handkerchief-hem dresses. Jeans were also acceptable as they continued their progress towards world domination.

Gradually, however, the Sixties obsession with space-age materials dissipated and designers returned to natural fabrics like wool and silk. Milan grew in importance, with knitwear by Missoni and fine wool separates from Krizia. Women enrolled in evening classes, learning how to crochet and knit their own waistcoats (made fashionable by Bill Gibb) to wear over trousers or evening dresses. In the United

In 1971, American actress Lesley Ann Warren wears a multicoloured
butterfly-wing kimono-style dress with fringed hem, by Cuban-born designer
Adolfo, teamed with red tights and sandals.

States, Bill Blass and Oscar de la Renta made elegant wool dresses and classic trenchcoats; and Diane von Furstenburg turned the wrap dress into her signature garment, which became an immediate classic.

Japanese designers making their mark in the early Seventies included Hanae Mori, Kenzo, Kansai Yamamoto and Issey Miyake, who mixed traditional Japanese features with cutting-edge techniques to produce theatrical outfits way ahead of their time.

Yohji Yamamoto and Rei Kawakubo (Comme des Garçons) would join the roll call of Japanese designers who would revolutionize fashion in the next decade.

Punk was the antithesis of glam rock and hippiedom. In 1974, Vivienne Westwood and Malcolm McLaren opened their boutique, Sex, on London's King's Road and started selling fetishwear; the shop became a magnet for the new punk kids on the street. Later McLaren would form the seminal punk band The

ABOVE These classic wool day dresses demonstrate that the flamboyant Seventies had a more reserved aspect, too.

OPPOSITE Debbie Harry, lead singer with the group Blondie, would become a style icon for many Seventies girls.

Sex Pistols from assorted King's Road habitués and visitors to the shop. Punk plundered street fashions of the previous two decades in a defiant gesture against the (by now ubiquitous) hippie style. Punks wore leather jackets ripped and stabbed with safety pins, loud tartan suits with bondage straps and T-shirts with pornographic or Nazi symbols. Young women exploited the aggressive look by wearing heavy make-up, tight black leather trousers and dominatrix heels.

Inevitably, mainstream fashion soon began to dilute the punk look. Zandra Rhodes' 1977 'Conceptual Chic' collection turned the ethos on its head by ripping ultra-feminine dresses and decorating them with real gold safety pins. As punk became a marketable concept, its power to shock diminished. Fashion, meanwhile, moved on to explore the next big idea from the street – a kind of fancy dress worn by the 'posers' or New Romantics.

ABOVE A model wearing brown checked skinny trousers by Levi's with a multi-coloured gingham man-styled shirt with large collar. The slimfit mohair jumper in autumnal stripes of black, white, chestnut and umber is by Hewlett Knitting Mills. The model's hair is in the high fashion page-boy style of the early Seventies.

LEFT Marisa Berenson, granddaughter of Schiaparelli, was named 'the Girl of the Seventies' by Yves Saint Laurent. She is seen here in a white maxidress by Gavroche, teamed with a snakeskin waistcoat by Ossie Clark. She wears an Yves Saint Laurent jacket over her shoulders, a tasseled suede hippie belt, a large medallion and Forties-style sandals by Halston.

OPPOSITE In 1970, actress Natalie Wood models a full-length hand-printed Zandra Rhodes chrome-yellow-and-scarlet felt voluminous dress with oriental banding detail and kimono sleeves.

ABOVE Artist, journalist and political activist Caroline Coon models white platform zip-up boots and a red-and-white hand-knitted graphic jumpsuit with tight hooped leggings and bloomer effect by Kansai Yamamoto in 1971. Yamamoto went on to design the Ziggy Stardust outfits for rock star David Bowie.

OPPOSITE Around 1971, a pulsating neon-orange and chocolate-brown crocheted tank-top is worn over an orange skinny-rib turtleneck sweater and brown herringbone miniskirt, all by Miss Pat. The brown leather belt is by Odyssey, the plastic bangle is by Kenneth J. Lane and the floppy hat is from Madcaps.

Matchpricks. Mad

OPPOSITE Around 1971, seated on a giant matchbook (smoking was fashionable in the Seventies), a model wears fuchsia-pink satin high-waisted flared dungarees with appliquéd black velvet hearts on the knees and derrière. The dungarees are held up by straps attached to a button on the waistband and are worn over a teal crushed velveteen long-sleeved skinny-fit tank top.

RIGHT Nicaraguan model and beauty (now human rights activist) Bianca Jagger arriving at Heathrow airport in style in 1972. She wears an Yves Saint Laurent white double-breasted tuxedo suit, black flare-collared shirt and bowler hat and carries a walking cane.

NOSTALGIA

The Seventies were a period of recession and social unrest in Britain. As times were hard, fashion designers began to look back wistfully at what they regarded as simpler times. With her natural fabrics and pretty prints, Laura Ashley is probably the best known of the English romantic designers (though she was in fact Welsh). Her name is synonymous with long, tiered cotton dresses with puffed sleeves, pin-tucks and high collars. These would often be worn under a floral pinafore, referencing a relaxed rural lifestyle that was far removed from the grim existence of the original peasants upon whom the outfits were based. This phenomenon has become known as 'milkmaidism'.

Bill Gibb produced sophisticated versions of romantic dresses with designs based on medieval and Renaissance costumes. He was the designer of choice for wealthy 'hippies'. Ossie Clark specialized in beautiful flowing dresses, often made with Celia Birtwell-designed fabric of chiffon or crêpe, with deep necklines and flowing bell sleeves. Clark's dresses may have looked as though they were designed for a fairy princess, but they were practical and modern and included a secret pocket for the essentials — a door key and a £5 note.

RIGHT In 1972, a model wears a belted V-necked cardigan dress of persimmon wool by Liz Claiborne over a primary-coloured graphic-print shirt with a long-winged 'tapered collar'.

OPPOSITE Singer, actress and daughter of Judy Garland, Lorna Luft wears a feathered fedora and 1971 tartan suit by Norma Kamali. The outfit pays homage to the Forties, though the midiskirt is longer and the ankle-strap platform sandals higher than the vintage originals. Kamali went on to invent the sleeping-bag coat and high-heeled sneakers.

BELOW In 1972, glamorous girl-next-door model Beshka wears a wasp-striped rugby shirt with white collar and cuffs and matching Hanes hosiery. Levi's for Gals rolled-up tight button-fly jeans, a studded leather belt and sunshine yellow clogs by Olof Daughters complete the look.

ABOVE A layered outfit of heather-coloured sweater, tights and tweed plus-fours, worn with a wool cloche hat and long fringed scarf; Guy Laroche's 1974–75 collection demonstrates the fashion nostalgia that prevailed in the Seventies.

OPPOSITE The world according to Missoni: around 1975, a model wears a multicoloured herringbone weave maxiskirt in the designer's trademark zigzag stripes. The matching striped top, floor cushion fabric and scarf tied as a turban over Thirties-style hair are also by Missoni.

LEFT Muse to Yves Saint Laurent, model and designer Loulou de la Falaise wears a floaty black, camel and coral stylized flower-print chiffon peasant mididress with filmy sleeves, matching scarf and gladiator-style silver sandals.

OPPOSITE In 1978, singer and actress Cher poses in a Bob Mackie ('the Sultan of Sequins') turquoise Spandex/Lycra bodysuit spangled with crystals and featuring a slashed bodice-laced front. Silver leather highwayman high-heeled boots underline Cher's status as the 'Goddess of Pop'.

BELOW Designer Vivienne Westwood (in tartan suit) seen here early in her career with other punks in London in 1977. Tartan, bondage straps, biker jackets, black clothing, safety pins and general artificiality were features of the punk street look popularized by Westwood and her partner Malcolm McLaren.

ABOVE Kim Charlton, photographed here in 1979 on her way to becoming a supermodel of the Eighties. She wears a Krizia plum, amber and gold thread checked wool Thirties-style twinset over a burnt orange wool-knit slit skirt by Walter Steiger for Pancaldi. The sheer tights and high black court shoes would become a staple of the Eighties daywear wardrobe.

OPPOSITE Seventies supermodel Gia wears a black velvet knee-length suit with puffed shoulders and peplum over a red-and-black jacquard silk blouse with a pussy-cat bow, all by Givenchy. Although this photo was taken in 1979, the styling hints at things to come in the largely monochrome Eighties.

The Exuberant Eighties

The decade began with Margaret Thatcher as British prime minister and movie actor Ronald Reagan about to become president of the United States. As a reaction to continuing economic uncertainty and the accompanying social unrest, nostalgically dreamy Ossie Clark/Celia Birtwell and Laura Ashley frocks became even more popular. But as the Eighties got into full swing, there was excitement (and trepidation) about the notion of a dawning Orwellian era. This futuristic anxiety was explored in a movie version of Orwell's famous novel *1984*. In fashion, the mood began to turn against prim florals and the 'prairie' ethnic hippie look. New Romantics congregated at the Blitz nightclub in London, took elements of romantic tradition, such as frilly fop shirts, quiffs and pallid makeup, and adapted them to eccentric, gender-bending effect.

Many New Romantics were students or unemployed, often living in squats, and they bought their clothing from jumble sales and theatrical costumiers. Boys typically wore full-sleeved ruffled-front blouson shirts with velvet knickerbockers, or they channelled David Bowie in wide demob trousers and tight jackets. Girls wore similar frothy blouses with pencil skirts or zouave pants. They also went for a Hollywood look in jumble-sale ballgowns and furs, or in dresses made by sewing two strips of brocade curtain together many times and pulling the threads to make a ruched tube. The remaining fabric was worn as a turban.

In 1981, Vivienne Westwood's first catwalk show demonstrated a New Romantic influence. In the same year, but at the other end of the style spectrum, the Emanuels went to town and back on Lady Diana Spencer's wedding dress, creating a lavish taffeta fairytale gown with an endless train. Entranced, the world watched the British royal wedding on television. The Emanuels' influence would be seen in bridal fashions for the rest of the decade.

Advances in technology and, specifically, the advent of the music cable channel MTV meant non-stop access to the latest pop videos. Consequently, the Eighties were a time of rapid crossover from pop to film/video to fashion. With her success both on MTV and in the movie *Desperately Seeking Susan*, pop artiste Madonna launched a new uniform of skirts over capri pants and fishnet tights, worn with crucifixes and fingerless lace gloves. A legion of young girls copied the look.

The fitness fad that had started a few years earlier took off in a big way, thanks to Jane Fonda's workout videos, the TV show *Fame* and the film *Flashdance*. Suddenly women with big hair were dressing as if for a Bob Fosse audition in leotards and skin-tight Lycra leggings under ra-ra skirts. These were worn with sloppy joe jumpers, or off-the-shoulder sweatshirts, and leg warmers – even at the height of summer! T-shirts were long, baggy and often emblazoned with slogans (courtesy of Katharine Hamnett). Jumpers with beading or sequins in geometric slashes were fashionable, particularly with aspiring 'Sloanes'. The trend for novelty sweaters was triggered by Princess Diana who in 1983 wore a sweater with a sheep design over a frilly blouse and long skirt, prompting an upper-class stampede to the separates store.

During the decade, as many women worked their way up the career ladder, fashion saw a business opportunity. The introduction of 'power' dressing led to the launch of tailored short-skirted suits with exaggerated, padded shoulders. The suits were

A Christian Lacroix outfit from his 1987 spring-summer haute couture line for Patou. The paisley blouse is worn with a white broderie anglaise skirt, crisscross-ribboned pink satin heels and a straw boater adorned with artificial fruit.

Vivienne Westwood, Malcolm McLaren (seated left and right) and
colleagues in the early Eighties at their shop in the King's Road, London.

usually made of pinstriped fabric, but sometimes
came in bold primary colours. They were worn with
high heels and a pussycat-bow blouse (a particular
favourite of Margaret Thatcher's). For city women,
an Armani suit was the ultimate in elegant
professional dressing.

This era also saw shoulderpads stuffed into
jumpers, jackets, dresses and even tracksuits, but
nowhere were they more prominent than in the
immensely popular American soap opera *Dynasty*.
As Linda Evans and Joan Collins exchanged
withering remarks in increasingly outrageous outfits

with extravagant trim and heavy-duty jewellery, a new word was coined – 'excessorizing'. Costume jewellery became wildly fashionable, with British duo Butler & Wilson's wittily opulent trinkets capturing the 'more is more' ethos.

The antithesis of the power suit came from Japanese designers such as Yohji Yamamoto, who draped monochrome fabrics around the body in a kimono-inspired, free-flowing form often decried as shapeless. Rei Kawakubo of Comme des Garçons took the Japanese influence to a new level with her radical, art-as-clothing pieces constructed inside out as a comment on clothing's place in society.

The exuberant Jean Paul Gaultier burst onto the fashion scene with his skirts for men, corset dresses – Madonna, with her 'underwear as outerwear' look, was a high-profile fan – and, more enduringly, his classic suits with double-breasted jackets worn over slim skirts or wide trousers. Both Gaultier and Vivienne Westwood were quick to interpret street fashion. They also combined good tailoring with glamour, a quality that makes their Eighties garments highly collectable today. Inevitably there was a backlash against the over-the-top look. Some young women took to dressing down pretty frocks by accessorizing them with socks or black opaque tights and 'Doc' Martens boots.

In a hint at the 'bling' that would become fashionable in the Nineties, rap and hip-hop fans dressed in designer sportswear, trainers and heavy gold jewellery. Towards the end of the decade, 'body-conscious' became a key look. Azzedine Alaïa created extremely tight-fitting stretchy dresses which, when worn with killer heels, became a defining look of the late-Eighties and Nineties and would endure well into the twenty-first century.

A black-and-white wool tweed coat with shawl collar and cuffs in beaver fur by Bill Blass, 1984. The black leather hat is by Patricia Underwood.

LEFT In 1981, model and actress Andie MacDowell wears a simple silk vest top and crêpe palazzo pantsuit under a punched gold sheepskin leather cardigan jacket – all by Jean Muir. The Kabuki kuroko character, played by Saeko Ichinohe, illustrates the interest there was in Japanese culture during the Eighties.

RIGHT Model Kelly Emberg in a navy blue double-breasted gabardine trouser suit of hip-length jacket with padded shoulders worn over a scoop-neck white silk crêpe-de-chine blouse. All the clothes are by Calvin Klein, the brown pigskin document case is by Mark Cross and the red quilted handbag is by Chanel.

BELOW Actress and model Isabella Rossellini, seen here in 1982, wearing a conker-and-cream pinstriped man-styled shirt with flame orange silk panels, gold silk cuffs and tie waist. The shirt and the toning cream-and-conker double pinstriped shorts and gold flat sandals are all by Armani. The striped acrylic bangle is by Cara Croninger and the typical Eighties large disc earrings are by Cathy and Marsha for Catherine Stein.

THE JAPANESE INVASION

The Japanese designers who came to prominence in the Eighties were a powerful antidote to the decade's mainstream fashions. New Romantic frills and flounces, aggressively tailored power suits and Lycra-and-legwarmer confections were challenged by developments in Japanese styling that elevated fashion to a form of modern art. Rei Kawakubo (Comme de Garçons), Issey Miyake, Kenzo and Yohji Yamamoto spearheaded a movement producing deconstructed clothing that referenced traditional Japanese costume. Fabric was draped, bodies wrapped and garments layered on top of one another to give a voluminous effect. Kawakubo said that her early Eighties designs were about shaking off the past: 'I felt I should be doing something more directional, more powerful. We had to get away from the folkloric.'

The texture, cut and drape of the fabric were more important than the colour, which was usually monochrome. Yamamoto described black as 'a colour both modest and arrogant'. Along with billowing fabric and precise asymmetric cutting, black was central to Yamamoto's revolutionary 'crow look' of 1981. Focusing on functionality and inventive anti-fashion, the Japanese design spirit of the Eighties still informs the world of haute couture today.

ABOVE Around 1983, American actress Brooke Shields poses in British stately home surroundings in a royal-blue silk crêpe and black velvet evening dress with puffed padded shoulders, long sleeves and thigh split by Oscar de la Renta. Her coat is from Anne Klein, the bracelet is by Fabrice for Montana, the earrings are by Cimabue and the handbag is by Carlos Falchi.

OPPOSITE Around 1982, model Christie Brinkley works out in a rose-pink Spandex unitard with carnation-pink legwarmers rolled down to the ankle. Big hair and lipgloss help to convey the brash, confident Eighties look.

LEFT Model, aristocrat and designer Inès de la Fressange on the runway for Emmanuelle Khanh's 1982–83 collection, wearing a long white cotton dress with layered train. Nostalgic and ethnic features abound in this garment with Victorian waist detail, off-the-shoulder ruff and Bedouin-style hood. Opaque tights, sandals and gloves complete the bright white theme.

RIGHT By 1985, the world had gone monochrome, discarding the hippie colours of the previous decade for a more sober, businesslike demeanour. From left to right: a Geoffrey Beene sleeveless, boat-neck, ballerina-length tube dress with evening gloves; an off-the shoulder, batwing, belted minidress by Calvin Klein; a strapless floor-length Oscar de la Renta evening gown with sash and fishtail; and a strapless silk taffeta cocktail dress by Jackie Rogers.

LEFT BOTTOM Diana Spencer, Princess of Wales and Eighties fashion icon in the colours of Canada during a state visit in 1983. Her red dress with puffed shoulders is topped by an enormous white lace Puritan collar with scalloped edging. She wears a matching white hat with red brim edge and band, accompanied by a simple pearl necklace and earrings.

OPPOSITE Eighties pop artist and material girl Madonna during her first concert in 1985. She wears a forest green cut-off top and miniskirt with a multicoloured boxy blazer over rolled-up blue lacy tights and green Victorian-style lace-up boots. Her boho rebel pose, complete with rosary and bare midriff, would quickly be appropriated by thousands of teenage fans.

RIGHT Singer, actress and model Grace Jones on the runway for Azzedine Alaïa's 1986 collection. Tunisian-born. Alaïa was dubbed 'the King of Cling' by the media for his body-skimming, seductive clothes. This cerise-pink shot silk evening dress has a side-tie detail, plunging neckline and incorporated hood, together with a fishtail and train. Worn with no jewellery, but plenty of attitude.

BELOW Christy Turlington, one of the great supermodels of the Eighties, in a Donna Karan long-sleeved navy wool crêpe jersey off-the-shoulder top with navy satin sarong skirt. Turlington also wears Estrada long-drop earrings, a Wendy Gell bracelet and silver strappy high-heeled sandals by Maud Frizon.

LEFT Japanese designer Kansai Yamamoto's 1986 ready-to-wear line included this avant-garde outfit of a white body shaper under a pink knee-length panel, worn over an apricot-and-cream chiffon underskirt. The matching hyacinth-pink bolero, which completes the layered look, has draped over-long sleeves. Accessories include a wide white belt, multicoloured sash and 'ethnic' hair braiding in ribbons *à la* Boy George, the British pop singer.

OPPOSITE A 1986 photograph of a Thierry Mugler short ivory silk shirtdress with padded shoulders, wide three-quarter-length sleeves and a slim, short skirt tied at the waist. Accessories include gold jewellery, pointed pumps and a large quilted document case.

BELOW Around 1986, this model wears a black dolman-sleeved turtleneck sweater tucked into wide ivory wool gabardine trousers with turn-ups and a slim black belt. The clothes, together with the pearl necklaces, bracelet and earrings, are all by Chanel. The slingback sandals and white scarf wrapped around the head are by Anne Klein.

ABOVE Supermodels Tatjana Patitz and Laetitia Firmin-Didot pose in outfits by Emanuel Ungaro. On the left, a slim knee-length pale skirt with diagonal stripes and slight bias cut is topped with a black-and-white loud-checked waisted jacket with rolled up sleeves and padded shoulders. On the right, a shorter straight scarlet skirt is worn with a checked jacket with back-tied belt and padded shoulders and a white turban.

LEFT Marpessa models a carmine-pink ruched-silk taffeta strapless evening dress with wired, wavy hem from Christian Lacroix's 1987–88 Paris show. In a typically dramatic flourish, Lacroix contrasts colour and texture with a jet-black velvet bikini-bodice and black net petticoats. Note the separate standout sleeves.

OPPOSITE In 1989, Jean Paul Gaultier's fringed bustier minidress maximizes the curves of Eighties supermodel Cindy Crawford. The frock has a red, black and gold Aztec pattern and a halter-neck feature and is worn with Diego Della Valle (of Tod's) metallic bronze high-heeled pumps.

Index